BY MARV ALINAS

Published by The Child's World®
800-599-READ • childsworld.com

Copyright © 2026 by The Child's World®
All rights reserved. No part of this book may be reproduced or utilized in any form or by any means without written permission from the publisher.

Photography Credits
© Aaron M. Sprecher/AP Photo: 12–13; Adam Hunger/AP Photo: 17; ChrisFloresFoto/Envato: football texture; Damian Strohmeyer/AP Photo: 6–7; David Zalubowski/AP Photo: 15; Greg Trott/AP Photo: 19; oasisamuel/Shutterstock.com: 6, 9, 14 (football); Richard Cavalleri/Shutterstock.com: 11; Ryan Kang/AP Photo: 4–5; Tom DiPace/AP Photo: cover, 2; Vernon Biever/AP Photo: 21

ISBN Information
9781503875241 (Reinforced Library Binding)
9781503875494 (Portable Document Format)
9781503876538 (Online Multi-user eBook)
9781503877573 (Electronic Publication)

LCCN
2024952251

Printed in the United States of America

ABOUT THE AUTHOR

Marv Alinas has written dozens of books for children. When she's not reading or writing, Marv enjoys spending time with her family and traveling to interesting places. Marv lives in Minnesota.

New York Jets wide receiver Garrett Wilson

CONTENTS

The Team 4

The Colors 6

The Conference 8

The Stadium 10

The Football Field 12

Fun Fans 14

The Coaches 16

The Players 18

The Future 20

    Fast Facts 22
    Glossary 23
    Find Out More . . . 24
    Index 24

The Team

The New York Jets are a football team. They play in East Rutherford, New Jersey. The team started in 1959.

The New York Jets run onto the field to play football.

The Colors

Their team colors are green and white. The Jets used to have cheerleaders called the "Flight Crew." The team does not have a **mascot**.

The Green Bay Packers, the Los Angeles Chargers, and the New York Giants also do not have mascots.

The Flight Crew cheered for the Jets from 2006 to 2022.

The Conference

The Jets are in the AFC East. The AFC stands for American Football **Conference**. There are three other teams in the AFC East.

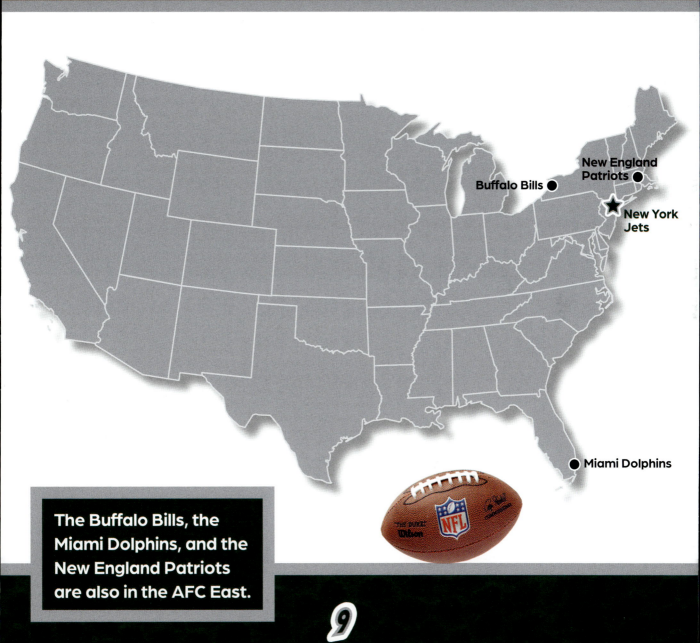

The Buffalo Bills, the Miami Dolphins, and the New England Patriots are also in the AFC East.

The Stadium

The Jets play at MetLife **Stadium**. It opened in 2010. It can hold more than 82,000 people.

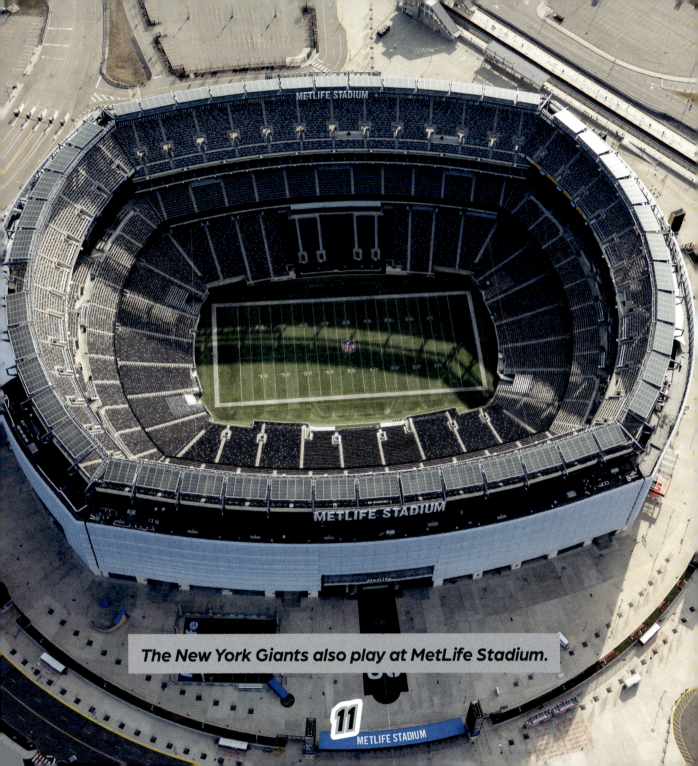

The New York Giants also play at MetLife Stadium.

The Football Field

Fun Fans

Jets fans love to wear the team's colors. Many people wear a **jersey** with the number of their favorite player. Jets fans can be very loud!

Fans love to shout "J–E–T–S, Jets, Jets, Jets!" after big plays.

The Coaches

The New York Jets have had 22 head coaches since they began. Aaron Glenn is the current coach. He became the head coach in 2025.

Aaron Glenn worked for other teams before the Jets.

The Players

Many great players have been part of the New York Jets. Some past greats include Joe Namath and Curtis Martin.

Current Jets stars are Garrett Wilson, Breece Hall, and Quinnen Williams.

Garrett Wilson runs with the ball during a 2024 game.

They are exciting to watch during games.

The Future

The Jets have gone to the **Super Bowl** one time. They won the game! They will keep trying for another win!

The Jets last won the Super Bowl in 1969.

FAST FACTS

- The New York Jets play in East Rutherford, New Jersey.

- The team is in the AFC East.

- MetLife Stadium can hold more than 82,000 people.

- The New York Jets have won the Super Bowl once.

GLOSSARY

conference (KON-fur-enss): In sports, a conference is a grouping of teams.

jersey (JUR-zee): A jersey is a shirt sports players wear.

mascot (MAS-kot): In sports, a mascot is an animal, person, or thing that represents a team.

stadium (STAY-dee-um): A stadium is a large building where sports and concerts are held.

Super Bowl (SOO-pur BOWL): The Super Bowl is the championship game of the NFL.

FIND OUT MORE

In the Library

Anderson, Josh. *New York Jets.*
Parker, CO: The Child's World, 2023.

Gigliotti, Jim. *The Story of the New York Jets.*
Minneapolis, MN: Kaleidoscope, 2021.

Scheffer, Janie. *The New York Jets.*
Minneapolis, MN: Bellwether Media, 2024.

On the Web

Visit our website for links about the New York Jets:
childsworld.com/links

*Note to Parents, Caregivers, Teachers, and Librarians:
We routinely verify our web links to make sure they are safe
and active sites. So encourage your readers to check them out!*

INDEX

colors, 6
conference, 8
East Rutherford, 4
fans, 14
field, 12–13
Flight Crew, 6

Glenn, Aaron, 16
Hall, Breece, 18
Martin, Curtis, 18
mascot, 6
MetLife Stadium, 10
Namath, Joe, 18

players, 18
Super Bowl, 20
Williams, Quinnen, 18
Wilson, Garrett, 2, 18, 19